SERIES EDITOR: MARTIN WINDR

MEN-AT-ARMS 351

BRITISH AIR FORCES 1914–18 (2)

TEXT BY
ANDREW CORMACK

COLOUR PLATES BY
PETER CORMACK

First published in 2001 by Osprey Publishing, Elms Court, Chapel Way, Botley, Oxford OX2 9LP, United Kingdom

E-mail: **info@ospreypublishing.com**

ISBN 1 84176 002 1

Editor: Martin Windrow
Design: Alan Hamp
Originated by Colourpath, London, UK
Printed in China through World Print Ltd

01 02 03 04 05   10 9 8 7 6 5 4 3 2 1

FOR A CATALOGUE OF ALL TITLES PUBLISHED BY OSPREY MILITARY AND AVIATION PLEASE WRITE TO:

The Marketing Manager, Osprey Publishing Ltd, PO Box 140, Wellingborough, Northants NN8 4ZA, United Kingdom
Email: **info@ospreydirect.co.uk**

The Marketing Manager, Osprey Direct USA, c/o Motorbooks International, PO Box 1, Osceola, WI 54020-0001, USA
Email: **info@ospreydirectusa.com**

BUY ONLINE AT:
www.ospreypublishing.com

Dedication

This book is dedicated to the staff, past and present, of the Royal Air Force Museum, Hendon, in tribute to their dedication and skill.

Author's Note

I am greatly indebted to the following individuals and institutions in the preparation of this book: Therese Angelo, Royal New Zealand Air Force Museum; Mrs Jean Buckberry, Librarian, RAF College, Cranwell; Sandra Coley, Shirley Collier; Kate Grainger; Mrs Margaret Laughton; Graham Potts; Flt Sgt Gil Singleton and Sgt Mark Willetts of the RAF Regiment Band, William Spencer, Military Specialist, Public Record Office; the British Library Patents Library; the Royal Air Force Museum.

Special thanks are due to my brother, Peter, for the colour illustrations and to my wife, Helen, for her patience, understanding and support.

Erratum

In Men-At-Arms 341 *British Air Forces 1914-1918 (1)* the Women's Army Auxiliary Corps is wrongly referred to as the Women's Auxiliary Army Corps.

Artist's Note

Readers may care to note that the original paintings from which the colour plates in this book were prepared are available for private sale. All reproduction copyright whatsoever is retained by the Publishers. All enquiries should be addressed to:

Peter Cormack, c/o 9A Woodside Lane, London N12 8RB, UK
Email: pdc@wolfofgubbio.freeserve.co.uk

The Publishers regret that they can enter into no correspondence upon this matter.

BRITISH AIR SERVICES 1914–18 (2) UNIFORMS OF THE RAF

THE ROYAL AIR FORCE

WHILST THE FOUNDING FATHERS OF THE Royal Flying Corps in 1912 had envisaged it as being a joint-service institution which would provide aerial support to both the Royal Navy and the Army this cherished hope had not lasted for very long. By the start of the First World War the Admiralty and the War Office had jealously gathered in their respective parts of the organisation. Once the fighting began the divergent viewpoints of the parent organisations naturally drew the two forces further apart and, though both achieved notable successes from the very beginning in Europe, Africa and the Dardanelles, their separation left a significant gap in matters of aerial defence at home. Both forces were naturally stretched to the limit of their capabilities as the scale of the war increased beyond expectation and, though efforts at co-operation were made, the lack of a central directing force continued to make itself felt. Though the Royal Flying Corps grew enormously in manpower and aircraft in comparison with the Royal Naval Air Service, such expansion was often not achieved in the most economical way, both in terms of human and material wastage. The War Office undoubtedly purchased aircraft that were unsuitable for their intended purpose and it certainly supplied squadrons with air crews whose training, though not their courage, left much to be desired. The Admiralty developed a better relationship with its aircraft suppliers, though of course both forces were competing for the same raw materials and engines, and the smaller size of the RNAS and its lower casualty rate gave its air crews a chance to acquire more air experience than those of the RFC. The development of the war during its first three years and the vast efforts it required to sustain its continued prosecution meant that the re-organisation of the air services was not at the forefront of the Government's mind.

The perceived success of the German airship campaign against the United Kingdom led to a re-appraisal of the British Air Services, both in relation to the defence of London in particular, and in respect of their general organisation for the prosecution of the war. General Jan Christian Smuts, the South African representative on the Imperial War Cabinet, was charged with looking into the situation and making recommendations to overcome the problems of Britain's air forces. His reports recommended a re-organisation of the home defences to address the immediate problem and an amalgamation of the air branches of the Navy and the Army to form a unified force providing aerial services to each. Though the proposal for a major re-organisation whilst the war was still in progress might be thought to be potentially

His Royal Highness Prince Albert, later HM King George VI, as a Major in the RAF Officers' khaki uniform. Ranks from Major to Colonel wore a single band of gold oak leaf embroidery on the cap peak. (RAFM P4060)

dangerous, the transformation was one of organisation behind the scenes and it did not have a drastic effect on the day-to-day business of the flying units. Nevertheless, the concept behind the change, the setting up of an independent third service dedicated to air warfare, was unique, radical and an inspired, though pragmatic, recognition of the enormous advances in aerial warfare in the few years since 1912.

The beginning of April 1918 did not, of course, herald a complete change of uniform for all those officers and men already serving with the RFC and RNAS. For non-commissioned ranks a gradual change-over was anticipated and regulations were published to regulate how the transformation should take place. Air Ministry Weekly Order (AMWO) 99 stipulated that until RAF patterns of uniform and badges became generally available men formerly of the RNAS and RFC would continue to wear what they possessed, but that when new issues were necessary no mixing of khaki and dark blue clothing was to take place: RNAS personnel would therefore be completely rekitted in Army General Service Pattern clothing, although it was permissible to wear khaki greatcoats with blue naval uniform. RFC clothing stocks would be used up and subsequent issues would be of GS Pattern kit. It was anticipated that GS jackets would be converted in unit tailors' shops to resemble the RAF pattern, but with the exception of changing buttons this rarely seems to have happened. The wearing of RAF, RFC or GS Pattern caps and greatcoats with any combination of khaki clothing was permitted. These

Second Lieutenant Bobby Burns with the very plain insignia of his rank at the cuffs and the gilt rank bars on his cap band. The shortage of gold embroidery wire has obliged him to purchase an all-metal cap badge of the type which was later allocated to Warrant Officer 1st Class. (RAFM H. Burns Colln)

sensible provisions led to a great variety of clothing being worn with what appear to be odd, though permitted, combinations of dress and badges.

The regulations for officers (AMWO 111) were somewhat different and, though a 'wearing out' period was allowed, they were not permitted to wear any promotions in rank that they received in the RAF on the uniforms of their former services. This therefore constituted a powerful encouragement to order the RAF patterns of clothing from their tailors as soon as promotion was achieved. Officers were however permitted to wear their old uniforms as working dress within the confines of their own aerodromes. In respect of both officers and airmen, photographs indicate that the conversion process did not completely work itself out of the system until 1920; in fact not until demobilisation had so reduced the force that a proper solution could be imposed on the problem. The new RAF uniforms for all ranks were regulated by Air Force Memorandum No. 2 (AFM 2), and its provisions, with the periodic amendments to it, will form the basis of this text.

Service Dress – Officers

Two uniforms were laid down for officers, both of exactly the same cut but in different colours; khaki and pale blue-grey. The latter was to be used as an optional Mess Dress only during the war. The

peaked cap had a fabric crown, black mohair band and patent leather peak and chin strap. The badge consisted of a crown above a gilt metal eagle with two pairs of laurel leaves below, all on a black fabric patch. The laurels were embroidered in gold wire and the crown in gold and silver wire with crimson velvet within the arches and coloured silks for the jewels. Additionally junior officers wore upright gilt bars on either side of the badge, a pair for Second Lieutenants and Lieutenants and two pairs for Captains. Field Officers wore one row of gold oak leaf embroidery on the cap peak, General Officers wore two. The **jacket** was a four-button single-breasted garment with lapels, no shoulder straps, a fabric belt fastening with a single-prong, gilt open frame buckle and a centre rear vent. It had straight flap and button bellows pockets in the skirt and pleated flap and button breast pockets, the flaps cut into three points. Buttons were gilt with a crowned eagle within a roped edge. Rank was indicated on the cuffs in three different widths of lace: broad 2¼ inches, standard ½ inch and narrow ¼ inch.

Rank	Broad	Standard	Narrow
General	1	3	
Lieutenant General	1	2	
Major General	1	1	
Brigadier General	1		
Colonel		4	
Lieutenant Colonel		3	
Major		2	1*
Captain		2	
Lieutenant	1		
Second Lieutenant	A crowned eagle on each cuff without lace.		

Lieutenant Robert Hughes Parry, Medical Officer, autumn 1918, in the pale blue uniform. The cuff eagles and cap rank tabs have disappeared, and he wears a maroon cap band and the large gilt collar badges of the Crux Anasata introduced by AMWO 1217 in October 1918. (RAFM P 8240)

* The narrow lace between the standard laces.

On the khaki uniform the lace was khaki with a pale blue centre stripe and on the blue version it was gold. Above these rings appeared a small gilt metal eagle with a separate crown above. The RAF continued to use Army rank titles until August 1919.

Khaki **trousers** and **breeches** of khaki or shades of fawn as in the RFC were worn with brown **footwear**, khaki puttees and shirts. In the pale blue uniform trousers only were to be provided, as breeches and puttees were not required for Mess Dress. They were worn with black shoes. The shirt was white and ties for both uniforms were black. The khaki British Warm **greatcoat** with rank on the shoulder straps was worn with both suits, no pale blue greatcoat was mentioned. Military-style waterproof coats were permitted. Brown leather gloves and walking sticks of various patterns completed the outfit.

The circumstances of officers transferring from one service to another and the difficult supply situation led very quickly to amendments being made to AFM 2. A shortage of gold embroidery wire obliged the sanction of two 'war economy' cap badges. Both had the three elements of crown, bird and laurel sprays, but the first had the three elements made in silver gilt and rivetted to a black fabric patch like the embroidered version (AMWO 83) whilst the second was struck in

The khaki 'British Warm' was acknowledged as the standard form of greatcoat for RAF Officers. Note the plain brown leather buttons. The crown and eagle that appeared above the rank lace on the shoulders was smaller than the equivalent cuff badge and was produced as one piece, not two separate pieces.

gilt-brass as a one-piece badge with crimson velvet panels clipped into the crown (Sealed Pattern No. 2080). This version was later restricted to officer cadets and Warrant Officers Class I in July 1919 (AMWO 783). Former RNAS officers in possession of black field boots were permitted to wear them with khaki clothing. In July 1918 (AMWO 617) the pale blue uniform was sanctioned for daytime wear as Service Dress, but was modified by the suppression of the cap band rank bars and the cuff eagles, Second Lieutenants henceforth wore a single narrow lace. Buttons on the blue uniform were no longer to have roped edges. Officers above the rank of Major General received a new cap badge of a crowned laurel wreath with a lion above, all in gold wire and colours, with a gilt eagle across the centre of the wreath. Breeches and puttees were added to the suit and a second prong to the jacket buckle. Blue or silver-grey shirts were permitted for working dress. Brown ankle or field boots could be worn. By October (AMWO 1140) all RAF officers were expected to have at least one suit of RAF uniform and former service uniform was definitively restricted to working dress. Cap band rank bars disappeared from the khaki uniform in the same month (AMWO 1318) and the crown and eagle cuff badge of Second Lieutenants was supplemented by a narrow lace of khaki and pale blue in December by AMWO 1597. The same order made it clear that officers were still wearing non-RAF uniform when off station and it forbade the practice, though at the same time allowing Army and dark blue naval greatcoats to be worn with RAF buttons. The first pale blue RAF greatcoat and a waterproof coat were sanctioned in mid-December. The greatcoat was double-breasted, longer than the British Warm and shaped at the waist with a belt and blue leather-covered buckle. The spacing of the three pairs of buttons tapered from 7 inches apart at the shoulders to 5 inches at the waist. The cuffs had three small buttons set vertically on the back seam. Soft shoulder straps, sewn down all round, carried gold rank lace and, probably, eagles. The raincoat was double-breasted with a belt, cuff straps, two flapped side pockets, but no shoulder straps. Rank badges were not worn.

The year 1919 saw few changes in officers' uniform. In July the general regulations were re-iterated and thereafter breeches were ordered to be khaki, the same colour as the jacket, not of a light shade. When wearing Service Dress for evening wear a white shirt was worn with both the blue and khaki uniforms (AMWO 783).

Cadets entering the RAF were to be graded Class A (Officers) or Class B (NCOs). Both Classes were intended for air crew training as pilots or observers according to aptitude. Class A was to be provided with a reduced kit of officers' clothing, Class B appears to have received GS Pattern kit. Photographs show that both wore white cap bands; Class A also wore officers' cap badges but no tabs and no rank insignia on the sleeve. Class B cadets seem often to have worn gilding metal numerals, presumably sub-unit numbers within their schools, instead of cap badges. In October, by AMWO 1319, all cadets were specifically instructed not to place orders for kit with tailors, presumably as it was clear that the war was coming to an end and the authorities wished to avoid the expense of re-imbursing grants. In the following year (AMWO 783) 'Other Cadets', presumably those formerly designated Class B, were to be issued with clothing of their rank, ie., WOII, Sergeant or Air Mechanic. All cadets were to wear white cap bands and either the embroidered officers' cap badge or the one-piece gilt metal version as for WOIs. No blue clothing was issued to cadets. Some schools had their own system of coloured patches and/or brass numerals worn on the upper sleeves and shoulder straps, but these are only ever seen on issued garments.

Service Dress – Non-Commissioned Officers and Airmen

Although all serving airmen continued to wear their former service clothing and, due to the supply situation, a good number of new entries were clothed in General Service Pattern garments, some stocks of the distinctive RAF uniforms were issued. All garments were khaki.

Warrant Officers Class I were clothed throughout in garments of officer pattern, but made up in Royal Army Clothing Department cloth. They used the same gold wire cap badge without gilt bars and their rank badge was the gilt eagle and separate crown worn on the upper sleeves. Ankle boots were brown. Warrant Officers Class II, NCOs and 1st, 2nd and 3rd Class Air Mechanics wore a **cap** with khaki crown and black band, peak and chin strap. All ranks wore a fabric cap badge consisting of a crown above a circular padded velvet 'cushion' encircled with two twisted threads and bearing an eagle in flight. For Airmen, the badge was embroidered in red worsted thread and for Corporals and all senior ranks in gold wire on a black background. The **jacket** was a five-button, single-breasted garment with a buckled fabric belt, stand and fall collar, no shoulder straps and cut with a panel back without vents. Sleeves had plain, stitched cuffs and there were patch pockets in the skirt with straight buttoned flaps and pleated patch pockets in the breast with buttoned flaps, which varied in shape according to the clothing contractor. The double-prong buckle and the crown, eagle and rope-edge buttons were described as being in bronze, though the Sealed Pattern has gilding metal examples. At the top of the sleeves, ranks below WOI wore red embroidered eagles with out-stretched neck and wings, the head facing backwards. Ranks were indicated on both arms according to the following table:

Lieutenant Humphrey Gerald Sullivan wearing one of the typical pale khaki raincoats permitted for Officers. Note the rank lace and gilt crowned eagle on the shoulder strap. Although wearing RAF uniform, Sullivan, who joined the Royal Naval Air Service in 1917, continues to wear his RNAS cap badge, probably because of the difficulty in obtaining an embroidered RAF one. (AC1998/27/1)

Rank	Badge
Warrant Officer Class II	Large crown above the cuff
Flight Sergeant	Three chevrons below a small crown on the upper arm
Sergeant	Three chevrons on the upper arm
Corporal	Two chevrons on the upper arm
Air Mechanics 1st Class	Twin-bladed propeller in red on the upper arm

Air Mechanic 2nd Class L.A. Goldsmith, 241 Squadron, photographed at Chesil Beach, Portland, wearing the khaki Jacket, Pattern 1918, Version 1. There were evidently contractors' variations in the cut of the breast pocket flaps and the generosity of the patch pockets in the skirts, some, like these, being gussetted. Buttons and buckle were gilding metal. Note the trouser turn-ups. (RAFM Album 00243)

Chevrons were of standard khaki Army lace and crowns were of pale drab embroidery. In 1919 (AMWO 24) 3rd Class Air Mechanics were abolished and the rank of Leading Aircraftman was introduced above 1st Class Air Mechanics. Thereafter Leading Aircraftmen wore the two-blade propeller and Air Mechanics wore no rank distinctions. By July 1919 (AMWO 783) the colour of their badge had changed from red to pale drab.

The suit was completed by standard serge **pantaloons**, puttees and trousers worn with brown boots. The **greatcoat** was described as 'the usual military type for Mounted Services' with shoulder eagles and rank badges worn as on the jacket. By July 1919 Warrant Officers Class I were instructed to wear the officers' pattern greatcoat, the British Warm, but without shoulder straps. The RAF Pattern greatcoat for all other personnel was a knee-length, double-breasted, eight-button garment with a wide falling collar, plain, leather buttons, inset flapped pockets at waist level and without a rear vent or half belt. Eagles, rank and trade badges were worn on both sleeves.

Photographic evidence indicates that this uniform was issued sparsely and it was never as common as the GS Pattern amongst airmen. However, for reasons that are not clear, it was superceded in October 1918 (AMWO 1268) by different patterns for all ranks and pictures show that these garments were extensively issued. Warrant Officers Class I, who must have been indistinguishable from commissioned officers at a distance in their first pattern uniform, received the jacket previously allocated to WOIIs and junior ranks. Their buttons, buckle and rank badges were definitely stated to be of gilding metal. All other ranks received a jacket with straight-flapped inset skirt pockets and single-point buttoned flaps on the pleated breast pockets. It had a buttoned belt and all buttons were of compressed leather moulded with an eagle, crown and roped edge.

The first version of the khaki clothing was not subjected to any official modifications, but it is clear that the shortage of gold embroidery wire lead to the introduction of a yellow worsted cap badge for WOIIs and NCOs, though it is never mentioned in Orders (Sealed Pattern No. 34, August 1918). In May 1919 all cap badges below WOI were changed to a gilding metal example similar to that of the RFC but with 'RAF' as the monogram within the crowned wreath (AMWO 545). In July WOIs received the one-piece gilt-brass cap badge formerly used by some officers. Photographs indicate that some Warrant Officers of both classes wore gilding metal Royal Arms or crown badges on khaki kit, presumably because of difficulties of supply. Some Air Mechanics, perhaps predominantly ex-RNAS personnel, indulged the habit of trimming down the rectangular patch on which shoulder eagles were embroidered and many were sewn on with the bird flying forwards rather than with its head facing backwards. Two completely unofficial badges are sometimes also seen on this clothing; the first is an initial **shoulder title** embroidered in pale drab on khaki with the letters 'R.A.F.'. The other is identical in form to the fully lettered RFC curved shoulder title, but reading 'ROYAL AIR FORCE' in two lines in off-white on black. The quality of the leather buttons on the second pattern jacket was so poor that many were fitted with gilding metal ones; a change which was officially sanctioned in 1922. Both brown and black footwear was permitted.

Although the wearing of khaki kit during the war was inevitable, the RAF's definitive uniform colour was pale blue and consideration was given early on to a set for Warrant Officers, NCOs and Air Mechanics. In July 1918 (AMWO 728) the pale blue **uniform** was announced as having been approved, though issue of it was deferred. It was similar to the khaki clothing with the following exceptions: WOIs were to use a gilt metal cap badge, whilst Air Mechanics had their worsted badge embroidered in pale blue; all ranks above Corporal wore four-button, single-breasted, fabric-belted, open-necked jackets with flapped, inset skirt pockets and pleated, buttoned breast pockets; buttons had no rope edging, buckles had two prongs. Shirts were silver-grey with black ties. Corporals and Air Mechanics had a pale blue version of their high-collar jacket, but with inset, flapped skirt pockets.

Sergeant Jackson wearing the Jacket, Pattern 1918, Version 2 with leather buttons and buttoned belt; Army of Occupation, Cologne, 1919. (RAFM Album 00198)

Warrant and non-commissioned officers of 241 Squadron, Portland Castle, autumn 1918. Naval, Army General Service Pattern and RAF uniforms are worn. The WOII wears a Sam Browne over a 1908 Pattern GS jacket and the Corporal Physical Training Instructor, rear row, wears the Army PTI badge of gilding metal crossed sabres. (RAFM Album 00243)

Rank badges and shoulder eagles, except for WOIs, were as for khaki, but in pale blue lace or embroidery on blue-black patches. WOIs were henceforth to wear the Royal Arms with supporters embroidered in pale blue on blue-black. Trousers, pantaloons and puttees were pale blue and footwear black. No greatcoat was included with the set.

Photographic evidence for the issue of this clothing is scarce, but it was certainly used by small groups of RAF personnel. It was modified in minor detail by AMWO 783 of July 1919, which introduced a blue shirt for WOs and Sergeants, and all ranks below WOI adopted the metal cap badge with this kit.

It is most likely that it was this blue kit which was authorised for general issue, but only for ceremonial and walking out purposes, by AMWO 1150 of 16 October 1919. Stocks of garments would, by that time, have been accumulated and, as the shade had already been changed in principle to blue-grey, it would have

Men of 21 Training Depot Station, Driffield, Yorkshire, February 1919. Mixed RFC, Army GS Pattern, RNAS khaki cap covers and RAF uniform is worn including the sergeant, centre, who wears the new pale blue uniform. (RAFM Photo Box 213)

been desirable to issue the obsolete colour so that it was used up.

With all these uniforms senior NCOs carried walking canes and Air Mechanics carried swagger sticks when parading without arms or for walking out. A wide variety was available, with or without metal caps, but in July they were regulated as brown for Warrant Officers and 'red', presumably a dull russet colour, for Other Ranks. Both had white metal tops bearing the RAF badge.

So serious did the manpower shortage become towards the end of the war that Boy Service was adopted by the RAF. It seems that boys were intended to be issued with exactly the same uniform as men, though it is most likely that they were clothed in GS Pattern kit. They were distinguished after July 1919 by a badge consisting of a four-blade propeller within a ring all in gilding metal worn on the upper left arm only of jacket and greatcoat. In 1923 this badge was re-designated as the Apprentice badge.

Badges

When the RAF was formed in 1918 it adopted the designs of the Royal Flying Corps flying badges for all qualified ranks. The observers' winged 'O' remained exactly the same and the pilots' wings merely changed the lettering within the wreath from 'RFC' to 'RAF'. For wear with the khaki uniform these badges were produced in off-white or pale buff embroidery, but when the blue uniform came into wear metal wire was substituted, observers having a gold wing with a silver 'O' and pilots having gold wings and wreath, a silver monogram and the crown in gold and colours. Both types appeared exclusively on black patches. The shortage of metallic embroidery wire which persisted throughout 1918 resulted in the production of silver gilt versions of these badges for wear on blue uniform. They were authorised in September by AMWO 1025 and were made in exactly the same way as the first 'war economy' cap badge with the elements rivetted to black fabric patches. The pilots' badge was made in three pieces and the observers' in two. All of these badges were worn by appropriately qualified crewmen of flying machines, whether land planes, flying boats, seaplanes, airships or kite balloons. They were intended for wear on RAF uniform only.

Air Force Memorandum No. 2 allotted a badge to Wireless Mechanics consisting of a hand clasping a thunderbolt with three flashes of lightning on either side. It was embroidered in red on khaki and worn on the upper arm above any rank insignia for Corporals and higher ranks, but below the Air Mechanic 1st Class badge. A pale blue on blue-black version was produced for the blue uniform. In August 1918 Air Ministry Monthly Order (AMMO) 747 introduced, in both colour combinations, a badge for Physical Training Instructors consisting of crossed sabres, points upwards, overlaid centrally by an eagle and with a crown between the sabre points. These two badges were worn on both sleeves of jackets and greatcoats. Medical staff were also distinguished. On the khaki uniform AFM 2 introduced a bronze Caduceus of Mercury as a collar badge for officers. This was discontinued in July by AMWO 727, but was replaced by a gilt Crux Anasata collar badge for all Medical Service personnel on both uniforms in October (AMWO 1217). In addition, this order introduced a maroon cap band for Medical Officers and the Geneva Cross arm badge – a red cross on a white circular ground with a dark blue edge – for Warrant Officers and all non-commissioned ranks. The position of this badge was clarified by AMWO 783 of July 1919 as being worn on both sleeves of jacket and greatcoat above all rank badges except those

Headquarters Staff, Palestine Brigade, 1918. Most of these officers wear RAF tropical uniform but the Major, centre, appears to have a white shirt and khaki tie and carries his rank on his cuff in the absence of shoulder straps. Note differences in footwear, leather buttons on the figures on the right, and KD caps or cap covers. (RAFM P1104)

of WOIIs, who wore it below the crown. Flight Sergeants wore their crowns above the Geneva Cross.

Personnel originating from the major countries of the Empire who were serving in the RAF were authorised to wear **shoulder titles** at the top of the sleeves. They gave the name of the country and were produced in gold wire on khaki or black curved patches for officers and Warrant Officers and in red on khaki or pale blue on blue-black for lower ranks. Badges were approved during 1918 for the following countries:

Country	Approval Order	Month
Canada	AMMO 747	August
South Africa	AMWO 1024	September
Rhodesia	AMWO 1365	October
New Zealand	AMWO 1668	December

In addition, personnel who had returned to Great Britain from South America were authorised to wear a special diamond-shaped pale blue badge with 'B' above 'L A' above 'V' (British Volunteer Latin America) within a narrow border all embroidered in yellow. This device was worn above the right breast pocket.

Initially the RAF continued the practice of wearing small, embroidered service **chevrons**, points upwards, on the lower right sleeve of jackets to denote service overseas or on ships since the start of the war. For khaki dress a red chevron was awarded for 1914 and blue chevrons for subsequent years. The latter were worn above the red one and the background patches for both were khaki. The qualifying periods for the award differed between the Army and the Navy, but service in the RAF after 1 April 1918 was not countable towards eligibility (AMWO 255). In July 1918 (AMWO 729) these badges were abolished on RAF uniform on the grounds that combatant service in the RAF was not restricted to those serving with Expeditionary Forces or in the Fleet. Most men who continued to wear their former service uniforms probably continued to wear them, those wearing RAF uniform should have removed them. In January 1919, however, these badges were re-introduced (AMWO 1). Service in the Army or Navy since 5 August 1914 was countable and continuous annual service in the RAF since 1 April 1918 was also countable towards the award. The colours of the chevrons changed, however, to pale green for 1914 and black for subsequent years. These colours applied to both khaki and pale blue uniforms, matching backing patches being produced for each. All ranks of the Women's Royal Air Force were also entitled to wear them.

Wound stripes in the form of 2-inch vertical strips of gold russia braid worn above the left cuff were worn with all RAF uniforms. A gilding metal

Lieutenant Colonel (later ACM Sir) Richard Edmund Charles Peirse, CO of 67 Wing, Taranto, Italy, June – November 1918. Absence of early instructions on tropical kit lead Peirse to have his jacket made exactly according to AFM 2 with rank insignia on the cuffs instead of on the shoulder straps. (RAFM AC71/13/20)

version of the badge fastening with lugs and a pin was also produced.

By September 1918 the RAF felt the need to form its own Police Department under a Provost Marshal. Policing duties on most units were dealt with under local arrangements, but for the very large establishments at Halton Park, Blandford, and in the Independent Force in France police controlled through the Air Ministry were deemed necessary. They were distinguished by a narrow black armband on the right arm bearing, in red embroidery, an eagle above the letters 'R.A.F.P.' arranged in a slight curve.

Working Clothing No Air Ministry Orders were issued covering this clothing and it is assumed that the RAF continued to use the brown and khaki overalls worn by the RFC.

Tropical Service Dress – Officers

Delays in the change of uniform from RFC/RNAS to the new RAF pattern were even more marked in the tropics than in Europe. Indeed it was not until June 1918 that AMWO 502 made any mention of tropical kit at all. Officers were advised that the approved pattern was to be the same as Service Dress, but made up in khaki drill fabric with detachable shoulder straps. The latter would carry rank insignia 'similar to that worn on the greatcoat' and, being detachable, they could be removed before the jacket was washed. Nothing is said about the other garments and it was evidently assumed that the rest of the kit was too well known to require description. It consisted of Wolseley helmet, shorts, trousers or breeches in KD fabric with sand-coloured shirts, black ties and brown footwear. Although very brief this order was fairly clear as regards the principal change and should have been easy to apply to newly-made kit. The use of the word 'similar' in the description of the rank insignia was unfortunate, as subsequent orders make it clear that it was intended that rank should be exactly the same as on greatcoat straps, namely khaki and pale blue rank lace with the one-piece gilt metal crown and eagle.

Where difficulties arose, however, were in the efforts officers made to convert the jackets they already had, and it is more common to see incorrect transformations than correct ones. Many officers continued to wear their Sam Brownes; some changed the buttons on their jackets but not the rank badges; some removed their old rank badges but applied the new lace to the cuff not the shoulder strap. Photographs indicate that the permutations were many and varied. It is quite clear that this situation persisted throughout the war and that the Regulations were only really conformed to after the War Service officers had come home and the Permanent Commission officers had had time to re-equip from the UK.

No major change was made to tropical kit by the consolidated restatement of dress regulations in AMWO 783 of July 1919, but it was

The wearing of non-standard tropical kit by Officers continued well into 1919. This lieutenant wears an Army-style jacket complete with rank pips and Sam Browne belt, but his crown and eagle buttons clearly show him to be in the RAF.

made clear that the gilt eagle badge on shoulder straps was no longer to be worn. It seems highly likely that few officers had in fact ever worn it.

Tropical Service Dress – NCOs and Other Ranks

No Weekly Orders at all were issued relating to tropical clothing for RAF NCOs and airmen during 1918. It is evident that the two- and four-pocket variants of the Army KD jacket as used by both the RFC and the RNAS continued to be worn with Wolseley helmets, Pith hats, KD trousers, pantaloons and shorts, KD or khaki puttees and black footwear exactly as during the previous four years. The new patterns of RAF shoulder, trade and rank badges reached foreign stations only slowly and the process of change was very gradual. Naturally this situation gave rise to some unauthorised adaptation and substitution and photographs indicate that this liberal tradition which had permeated RFC/RNAS dress was kept alive in the new service.

As late as July 1919 AMWO 783 said nothing more than that the patterns of the major garments for all Warrant Officers and non-commissioned ranks were to be 'as authorised for the Army'. However, photographs and a few existing garments indicate that this was not universally the case. The second version of the 1918 Pattern jacket for Other Ranks with a buttoned belt was certainly made and issued in KD fabric with red on KD shoulder eagles. Some Warrant Officers Class I conformed to the spirit of AFM 2 and wore jackets of officer Home Service style, but with false pointed cuffs, on which they wore crown and eagle metal badges on the upper arm. In these cases shirts with soft collars were sand coloured and ties were black.

The imposition of truly uniform tropical clothing within the RAF was not achieved until the mid-1920s.

Senior NCOs at Murree Hills, North-West Frontier Province, India, late 1919 – a photograph on which one could write a whole article. Note the two- and four-pocket jackets with large and small buttons on each type, the Wolseley and Pith hats all with RFC flashes, the metal RAF shoulder title, and the three Warrant Officers Class I and the variations between their jackets. (RAFM Album 00039)

THE WOMEN'S ROYAL AIR FORCE

The successful introduction of large numbers of women to the military life which the foundation of the Women's Army Auxiliary Corps and the Women's Royal Naval Service had demonstrated meant that there was no hesitation by the Air Ministry in adopting female personnel within the Royal Air Force. All ranks of both women's forces serving with RFC or RNAS units on 31 March 1918 were given the option of transferring to the WRAF up to 1 May. Members of the Women's Legion Motor Drivers, which had continued to provide MT support to the RFC in the United Kingdom after the formation of the WAAC, could opt to transfer to the WRAF before 14 April or remain attached to the Army and receive a posting to the Army Service Corps.

As with their male colleagues there was no immediate change to the uniforms of Members or Ratings on the establishment of the new service and rather less in the way of adaptation than might have been anticipated. It is very rare to see any change at all in the clothing worn by Ratings of the WRNS. This was probably because they continued to serve at naval airship stations and as the airships remained under naval charge there was little pressure to change. In addition the durable WRNS uniform had only recently been issued so there was still a considerable period before it could be worn out. In any case the new khaki items of uniform could not be worn with WRNS clothing. The same was not, however, the case with WAAC uniform and it is interesting to note that the uniform for WRAF Members was produced in a similar shade of rather greyish khaki to that used for the WAAC coatfrock. There was thus no aesthetic conflict in wearing compatible items from the two sets and to some degree this did happen. It is quite common to see photographs of women wearing WAAC coatfrocks, and WRAF caps and WRAF Subordinate Officers' 'rank' badges also appeared on coatfrocks. The descriptions below, however, relate to the official clothing introduced as WRAF uniform.

The Officers of the WRAF School of Instruction, Berridge House, Hampstead, London. The difference in shade between the pale blue and khaki uniforms shows up very well. (RAFM X001-2616/001)

Service Dress – Officers

No full description of the dress for officers of the WRAF ever appears to have been issued, though details of insignia are included in FS Publication No. 32. In essence they wore a jacket identical to that of RAF officers, but cut for the female figure and worn with skirts. It seems that the clothing was produced in khaki first and that pale blue was adopted at the same time as it was approved for wear as Service Dress by RAF officers. Gilt crown and eagle buttons appeared on both suits; rope edged for khaki and without an edge for blue. Small clothes – shirts, ties, gloves and footwear – conformed in colour to those worn by RAF officers, and stockings were brown for the khaki uniform and black with the blue one. The WRAF officers' cap differed in form to that worn by WAAC Officials, having a close-fitting, gathered fabric crown overlaid with an oval fore-and-aft panel, a black mohair band and a semi-stiff fabric-covered peak retained in shape by multiple rows of stitching. A turned-up rear peak was provided and a black patent leather chin strap. The standard RAF officer's cap badge appeared at the front.

Rank insignia in April 1918 consisted of a combination of khaki and pale blue laces and buttons on both cuffs which distinguished 'Grades' of Officer which were simply numbered. The widths of lace are referred to as 'double' and 'single', though these were exactly the same as RAF broad and standard laces.

WRAF Officer in her khaki greatcoat to which she has added a fur collar, which obscures the absence of shoulder straps. She also wears wide-cuffed fur gauntlets. (RAFM Album B29)

Rank	Broad	Standard	Buttons
Grade 1	1	1	1
Grade 2	1		3
Grade 3	1		2
Grade 4	1		1
Grade 5		2	2
Grade 6		2	1
Grade 7		1	3
Grade 8		1	2
Grade 9		1	1

FS Publication No. 32 says that for Grade 1 the lace was surmounted by the button, but a surviving example of a Grade 9 jacket shows the small-size button in the centre of the cuff below the lace. Though very rarely seen in photographs, this style of rank insignia lasted until October 1918 when, by AMWO 1254, both rank titles and badges were changed according to the following table:

Title	Broad	Standard	Narrow
Commandant	1		
Deputy Commandant		4	
Assistant Commandant Class I		3	
Assistant Commandant Class II		2	1
Deputy Assistant Commandant		2	
Administrator		2	
Dep. Assistant Commandant (Staff)		2	
Deputy Administrator		1	
Superintendent		1	
Quartermistress		1	*table continues opposite*

OPPOSITE **A fine study of a chief section leader of the Immobile Branch wearing the khaki single-breasted uniform. (RAFM Box 171)**

A fine mixed group of RAF in both versions of the 1918 khaki jackets and WRAF in the single-breasted and the flap-over types in pale blue. The central figure has added a chin strap to her cap. (RAFM Box 171)

Title	Broad	Standard	Narrow
Assistant Administrator			None
Assistant Superintendent			None
Assistant Quartermistress			None

In the khaki uniform the laces were surmounted by the gilt eagle and crown and the three most junior 'ranks' wore cuff eagles and crowns only, the same as RAF Second Lieutenants, until December 1918. Assistant Commandants Class II wore their narrow lace between the standard ones like Majors. When wearing the blue uniform with gold rank lace the WRAF conformed to AMWO 617 by removing cuff eagles and adopting a single narrow lace for the three most junior ranks. By November 1918 these ranks had been further consolidated and simplified. The titles of address, with their RAF equivalent ranks, were Commandant (Brigadier General), Deputy Commandant (Colonel), Assistant Commandant Class I (Lieutenant Colonel) or Class II (Major), Administrator (Captain), Deputy Administrator (Lieutenant) and Assistant Administrator (Second Lieutenant).

A greatcoat was mentioned in FS Publication No. 32 and photographs indicate that it was khaki, double-breasted and had a gilt, buckled belt. It was specifically stated that no rank badges were to be worn on it, so it seems unlikely that it had shoulder straps. When a pale blue-grey greatcoat was introduced for RAF officers in December 1918, it is assumed that a similar garment was permitted to WRAF officers. Officers were allowed to wear gaiters in either brown or khaki with the khaki uniform and black with the blue clothing.

No changes were made to WRAF officers' uniform during 1919.

Service Dress – Members

Even during the war it was recognised that the uniform that had been produced for the Women's Army Auxiliary Corps was not a satisfactory

WAAC clothing remained in use with the WRAF well into 1918, particularly in the UK. Two chevrons denoting a section leader were adopted in November 1918, and this young woman still wears her RFC shoulder titles eight months after the Corps was absorbed by the RAF. (RAFM Album B29)

set of garments for military service. The WRAF was very fortunate in the clothing it received, as it was practical, sufficiently warm in most circumstances, smart with a military air and very well manufactured from much higher quality fabrics than one would expect. As with the officers no descriptions of the dress seem to have been issued in orders, but it is well known from surviving examples and photographs. The garments were produced in two colours, a rather greyish khaki and pale blue-grey, and were made up in a whipcord-type fabric rather than the WRNS serge or the light twill of WAAC clothing.

The **cap** was an all-fabric affair with a soft crown gathered into a band of the same colour with a semi-stiff peak supported by multiple rows of stitching and a plain rear peak, normally worn turned up. There was no chin strap. On the band Members and Subordinate Officers wore the same design of cap badge as used by the RAF, but embroidered in white on black. The **jacket** came in two styles which seem to have been issued indiscriminately, women in the same unit wearing both styles regardless of age, trade or figure. The first was a four-button single-breasted garment with a roll step collar and lapels, two large flap and button gussetted external pockets in the skirt and a two-button fabric belt retained in loops at the rear of the body. These buttons were arranged to fasten equally spaced either side of the centre opening. The cuffs were plain and there were no shoulder straps. This jacket, in either colour, was worn with a white shirt and black tie. The second pattern was reminiscent of the RFC tunic and was cut with a broad flap extending to the left shoulder and fastening with five visible buttons. It had a low falling collar cut in a V at the front and fitted with a false white collar inside which showed a half-inch strip round the neck, a single buttoned belt which fastened in line with the other buttons on the left and two pockets in the skirt. Like the other pattern these had straight buttoned flaps, but the pocket bag was inside the coat, only the flap showing on the outside. Both jackets were cut with ample fabric in the body which had to be arranged evenly round the waist when the belt was fastened. Buttons were of gilding metal with a crowned eagle and no edge.

Shoulder titles were worn at the head of the sleeve bearing 'W.R.A.F.' in white embroidery on black curved patches and on the upper arms were eagles in the same colours. Unlike RAF shoulder eagles, which were on rectangular patches, those for the WRAF conformed to the shape of the embroidered device having a 6mm border all round. Subordinate Officers were distinguished by large **arm badges,** which replaced the eagles on both sleeves; Chief Section Leaders (Sergeant equivalents) wore an eagle within a horizontal oval wreath with a crown above and Section Leaders (Corporal equivalents) wore the wreathed eagle without a crown. These badges also were in white on black. All eagle badges were made in pairs and the eagles were to be positioned with the heads extending backwards. Skirts of mid-calf length worn with khaki or black stockings and black laced shoes completed the outfit.

Field Service Publication No. 32 makes it clear that most WRAF Members were not intended to be issued with **greatcoats** and were instead to receive a 'Coat, Waterproof, WRAF Pattern'. This garment was double-breasted with five large, plain, crown and eagle buttons on the left and four on the right. It was normally fastened with only three when the lapels were turned back. It had a two-button belt, a falling collar, horizontal flapped internal pockets and no shoulder straps. There was a vent at the rear closed by two small uniform buttons and one of these appeared on the left lower skirt to keep the opening closed in foul weather. It fastened to a concealed tab inside the right front. The collar could be worn turned up and retained by a tab normally hidden beneath the right side. No badges were worn on this coat. Its issue was almost certainly an acknowledgement that the good quality jacket and skirt kit gave sufficient comfort in all normal circumstances and probably indicates that the WAAC greatcoat was worn more commonly than was strictly convenient by inadequately-dressed personnel whose coatfrocks were insufficient to keep them warm. By up-grading the basic suit for the WRAF the need for a heavy outer garment was obviated.

The exception to this rule was those personnel employed as motor transport drivers, who received a special WRAF Pattern khaki greatcoat which fell to mid-calf. It was single-breasted with five leather buttons, a broad collar and an all-round belt fastening with two closely spaced buttons. There were flapped pockets in the skirt and no shoulder straps. Another overcoat also appears in photographs. It was the same general shape as the Greatcoat and, though single-breasted, its buttons were set slightly to the wearer's left. It had two buttons set high on the breast to retain the lapels when folded back and it had a buckled belt. It may be the garment designated the 'Coat, Motorcyclist'.

Badges
Apart from the badges of rank dealt with above, WRAF Members belonging to the Immobile Branch were distinguished by a large white capital letter 'I' on a black rectangular patch worn above the eagle badge on both sleeves. Immobiles were personnel recruited from the locality of an RAF station who resided at home, travelling to work each day. Their terms of service did not permit them to be posted to another station. The only trade to be distinguished by a special badge was that of Mechanical Transport Driver for whom 'MT' embroidered in white on a black patch was produced. No regulations governing its use appear to have been issued and photographs of MT personnel with their vehicles do not show it being worn. It is presumed that it was an arm badge. As stated earlier, the WRAF was permitted to wear the War Service chevrons introduced by AMWO 1 of January 1919.

The changes that took place to both sets of clothing exclusively affected the badges worn on them. Khaki clothing was gradually replaced with blue, but it is clear from photographs that WAAC clothing continued to be worn by some Members with WRAF badges until at least the winter of 1918. In November 1918 the

Member Aylmore-Ayling wears pantaloons and boots for her motorcyclist duties. Her sleeves carry both the shoulder title and the eagle. Her gauntlets and boots both appear to be brown to tone with the khaki uniform. (RAFM P032471)

The single-breasted WRAF uniform in pale blue. The generous cut of the jacket is not matched by the length of the belt, which is obviously too short for this lady.

Subordinate Officers' rank structure was changed by the addition of Sub-Leaders, though no rank badge was announced for them in AMWO 1394. A fortnight later, by AMWO 1496, the badges of all Subordinate Officers were altered and became the standard chevrons in khaki or pale blue – 3 for Chief Section Leaders, 2 for Section Leaders and 1 for Sub-Leaders. It took a considerable time for the attractive eagle and wreath badges to be replaced by these less ornate patterns. In January 1919 a further rank was added to the structure in the form of Senior Leaders, who were the equivalent of Warrant Officers Class II. They wore the same insignia, an embroidered crown, on both lower sleeves. Late in February it was announced that the WRAF shoulder titles were to be abolished and henceforth the eagle badges were to be worn at the top of the sleeves. In May the embroidered cap badge was ordered to be replaced by the gilding metal badge exactly as introduced for WOIIs and all lower ranks of the RAF.

Working Clothing

As with the WAAC and the WRNS a range of working and foul weather clothing was available to the WRAF. Few photographs exist of it being worn and the precise patterns in most cases are therefore a matter of conjecture. Included in kit lists were various types of overalls or boiler suits; motor dust coats; caps, jean – probably a form of small, triangular head scarf; clogs for domestics (kitchen workers); rubber aprons for MT drivers and domestics; fabric aprons for kitchen workers and nursing staff; oilskin sou'westers, jackets and trousers; leather jerkins; gardeners' smocks; leather leggings; heavy boots and rubber gum boots. In addition Members engaged in medical duties wore 'caps' of Sister Dora pattern and were specifically forbidden to wear the head veil of the RAF Nursing Service. Sun curtains to cover the nape of the neck were authorised for wear by MT drivers in August 1919. From the start this latter group was provided with a brown, fur-lined, leather peakless cap for wear in cold weather.

ROYAL AIR FORCE NURSING SERVICE

Shortly after the formation of the RAF it became clear that the new force would become responsible for certain hospitals entirely independent of those run by the Army, and would therefore require its own nursing organisation to staff them. These hospitals were all located in the UK and casualties in France and elsewhere continued to be dealt with by the

One of the WRAF waterproof coats. Note that though single-breasted it buttons off-centre and has two buttons to allow the lapels to be fastened across. The buckle appears to be leather-covered. (RAFM PC1998/164/24)

medical staffs under Army control. By July 1918 a Matron-in-Chief had been appointed with an assistant and the question of uniform was being tackled along with other matters. In the almost total absence of photographs showing the uniform at this period the following description is based upon documents of the period and photographs of those garments which continued in use after 1920 when the collar and hat badges changed.

It was decided very early on that the RAF Nursing Service should wear the same shade of pale blue-grey as had been chosen for the RAF's definitive uniform. The fabric type chosen was the light-weight whipcord used for officers' caps. The first proposal envisaged a dress of RAF coloured material of unspecified composition faced with RAF-cloth and braided for the Matron-in-Chief and an RAF-blue straw bonnet. Matrons were to have winter and summer uniform dresses and cloaks of different weights, muslin caps, collars and cuffs, a shoulder cape and a bonnet. Sisters had the same dresses and 'muslins' plus blue cotton washing dresses, aprons, capes and winter and summer three-cornered hats in felt and straw respectively. Staff Nurses wore the same but without hats. In the context of nursing uniform muslin 'caps' meant a large square of fabric, folded and pinned round the head so as to form a triangular head veil. Waterproof trench coats in RAF blue and caps, presumably of the same design as the WRAF officer's cap, were permitted as optional garments, however, no specific provision was made for outdoor inclement weather wear for Sisters and Staff Nurses.

Though this wardrobe was modest, the £8 grant originally allowed by the Treasury for its purchase was wholly inadequate to cover the cost. Despite this difficulty, practical thinking had added a jacket to the list for all Members by September. In the same month the shape of the hat was changed to a four-cornered type so as to avoid causing any ill-feeling with the officers of the Women's Royal Naval Service who already used a tricorne. The first twenty appointments to the RAFNS were made at the beginning of October 1918 and during the winter practical experience dictated the necessity of adding warmer outdoor clothing to the kit list, which was finally settled in January 1919.

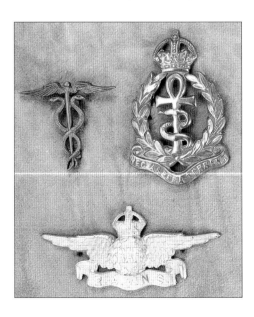

Medical badges: (left) Caduceus of Mercury, Pattern 1918, bronze, worn by Medical Officers on khaki uniform; (right) Crux Anasata, Pattern 1918, gilding metal, worn by MOs and Orderlies on both uniforms. (Bottom) RAF Nursing Service hat badge, 'all gilt'. The same badge, slightly smaller, was worn on the cape and jacket collar.

Due to financial stringency the garments purchased by members were those intended for winter uniform wear and essential working clothing. Indoor uniform consisted of the white head veil worn with the 'cloth' dress, which had long, close-fitting sleeves and a shallow stand collar and was worn with a narrow muslin collar and cuffs tacked in position. It had a narrow fabric belt which fastened with concealed hooks and

Matron Joanna Cruikshank, RAF Nursing Service. The only known photograph of a member of the RAFNS wearing indoor uniform with the cape embellished with the service's special badge. (Courtesy Mrs M. Laughton)

eyes and had eight gilt buttons from throat to waist. It extended to mid-calf and was worn with the shoulder cape. This garment fastened at the base of the neck with a concealed hook and eye, fell to the elbow and was cut with a broad, self-coloured facing all round and, almost certainly, a rosette at the centre rear on the facing. Small 'all-gilt' badges consisting of 'RAF' within a crowned wreath between wings supported on a decorative scroll bearing 'R.A.F.N.S.' were worn across the front corners. The outfit was completed by black stockings and lace-up black shoes. Sisters and Staff Nurses when actually nursing patients wore long-sleeved 'washing dresses', which seem to be pale blue in colour. They were fitted with large, starched stand-and-fall collars and cuffs and were always covered with voluminous bib-fronted aprons. The shoulder cape was worn with this ensemble when not actually in the wards.

Outdoor uniform was worn when away from the buildings and immediate grounds of the hospital. The black felt four-cornered hat was retained in shape by short tapes sewn between the brim and the domed crown. Only the outer edges of the brim were turned up leaving much of the crown visible. It had a black mohair band and bow and carried a larger version of the shoulder cape badge described above. The precise position of the bow and badge on the hat is unknown. The bonnets intended for all Matrons proved to be too difficult to produce in the pale RAF blue-grey colour and far too expensive. They were, therefore, never introduced. Matrons adopted the hat that was also allowed to Staff Nurses. Over the uniform dress all grades wore a Norfolk jacket fastening with three gilt buttons and a two-buttoned belt. Its most distinctive features were broad, vertical bands of fabric stitched down the front and back of the coat in line with the points of the collar bone. At waist level these bands were left open for the belt to pass through. The jacket had lapels and inset pockets with flaps positioned at the sides of the jacket skirts so as not to interfere with the bands. The small RAFNS badges were worn on the collar.

It was admitted in January 1922 that no Air Ministry Weekly Order had been issued up to that time stating officially the badges of the various grades nor had any approved pattern of 'rank braid' been sealed. A document of January 1919, however, makes it clear that 'rank' was shown in black braid; Matrons wearing two rings of ⅝ inch (15mm) braid on each sleeve, Sisters one ⅝ inch braid and Staff Nurses one ⅜ inch (9mm) braid. These distinctions seem to have been worn on both types of dress and the jacket. On the washing dresses they were certainly worn on the mid-forearm above the starched cuffs. The same document mentions a cloak for Matrons as well as a waterproof trench coat and a winter coat – a greatcoat – for all grades. The patterns of these garments were the same as those for WRAF officers but fur collars were forbidden. No jewellery or ornaments were to be worn.

FLYING CLOTHING

Captain Gilbert William Mapplebeck wearing a Warren helmet at his training unit. Goggles could be worn with this head-dress but it was not well adapted to them. (RAFM X001-6550-018-008)

Whilst little systematic development had taken place in garments specifically for flying since it became a popular, though very exclusive, activity around 1910, some consensus had emerged amongst the aviation fraternity by 1912 which provided a little direction to the authorities as to what they should provide for military aviators. The first pilots adapted civilian clothing or adopted motoring clothes, and from the latter the dominance of leather in early flying kit originated. There was also some acknowledgement of the convenience of wearing combination, overall-type garments which would bear fruit later on. More thought had been put into head-gear and some protective helmets had been designed, but many civil pilots still flew with a tweed cap turned backwards so that it did not blow off. This lack of development was not at all surprising as flying was a short-duration, good-weather, low-altitude leisure activity devoid of the imperative of military duty. Once it became part of soldiering, different factors applied and the subject was addressed more seriously.

The problems facing aviators all derived from the speed of flight – the chilling breeze created by passage through the air, known as slip-stream. Speed also brought with it the need to protect the head from injury in case of mishap and the eyes from dust, exhaust particles and oil caught up in the slipstream. As military aviation developed, the imperatives of operational service overrode the early constraints as to altitude, duration and weather. At the same time the activities additional to merely piloting an aeroplane increased. The combination of these factors influenced the development of flying clothing, at least as far as the capabilities of the available materials would permit. Whilst it is not the purpose of this book to examine in detail the development of military aviation, it will be useful to indicate some of the functions of pilots and observers other than pure flying.

From the first Army manoeuvres in which aeroplanes participated in 1912, air crews had to navigate, map-read, observe accurately movements on the ground and produce reports and sketches, packing them in

Second Lieutenant Brian Baker (left) and Flight Sub-Lieutenant George Gray (right) wearing the long lappet-type helmet. Note the slit in the right lappet of Baker's helmet, the retaining loop and the bow on top of Gray's. (RAFM RAeC 1938 & 2268)

Sergeant Frederick James Shaw wearing a fabric-lined cap with no ear rolls, which is possibly the official issue Cap, Leather Pattern 1915. Note the hook and eye fastener on the elastic throat strap. His goggles are the official issue all-rubber type. (RAFM RAeC 3366)

containers to drop them over headquarters. During 1914 the requirement to operate hand-held firearms in the air appeared, and from 1915 machine guns commonly came into use, necessitating the ability to clear stoppages in the weapon and to replenish its ammunition supply in the form of detachable magazines. The introduction of wireless telegraphy and reconnaissance cameras using glass plate negatives, also required the accurate and fast manipulation of these gadgets in a craft often bumping about in response to anti-aircraft fire or weather conditions. Coupled with this expansion of the functions of air crews was a gradual increase in the speed of aircraft and a dramatic increase in the altitude at which these tasks were performed. Increased altitude meant increased cold; a loss of 2 degrees centigrade for every 1,000 feet. By 1917 fighter operations were frequently carried out at heights around 15,000 feet, and from 1916 defence against Zeppelin raiders necessitated flying at night. This combination of factors imposed a considerable strain on the air crews and on the type of clothing that they wore. Their courage met the challenge, but only by the war's end was their clothing near matching it.

Although before 1916 officers entering the Royal Flying Corps were required to have taken their pilot's certificate, this was no guarantee that they would be in possession of any but the most basic flying clothing. Passengers in aircraft would certainly not have had such kit and, whilst officers would have the means to buy it, Other Ranks almost certainly would not, particularly if their duties aloft were occasional rather than regular. From 1912 the War Office provided a range of kit on issue and, as the force was at this time still a joint-service organisation, this clothing was used by both Naval Ratings and Army Other Ranks. After July 1914 when the RFC and RNAS formally separated and particularly after the war began, commercial companies produced a wide range of garments to cater for the large market amongst officers purchasing their own kit. As there was so little experience on which to base the design of these garments their claims to be 'just the thing' for the newly fledged aviator should be taken with caution. For those who survived long enough, experience doubtless taught them what was truly practical and what was merely showy.

The prevalence of private purchasing by officers makes it very difficult to be certain what was Official Issue kit and what was commercial. In addition it is clear that the War Office purchased clothing from the trade for supply to its aviators, much of this not being marked with issuing stamps. Where possible garments that were definitely issued will be described, but it is clear that identical garments were available privately. The self-kitting expected of officers also manifested itself in the widespread, but by no means universal, adoption of black leather flying kit by RNAS officers in breach of Regulations which stipulated brown.

(continued on p33)

1: Lieutenant, RAF, spring 1918
2: Captain, RAF, Medical Officer, winter 1918-19
3: Second Lieutenant, RAF, spring 1918

A

1: Air Mechanic 1st Class, Wireless Mechanic, late spring 1918
2: Corporal, RAF Police, 1919
3: Bandsman, 1918

B

1: Warrant Officer Class I/Sergeant Major, summer 1918
2: Warrant Officer Class II; Russian Intervention campaign, winter 1918-19
3: Sergeant, Physical Training Instructor, autumn 1918

1: Lieutenant, RAF, formerly RNAS; Mediterranean, summer 1918
2: Flight Sergeant; Egypt, 1918
3: Captain, RAF, formerly RFC; Egypt/Palestine, 1918

1

2

3

D

1: Chief Section Leader, WRAF, Motor Transport, winter 1918
2: Sister, RAF Nursing Service, Outdoor Uniform, October 1918
3: Sub-Leader, WRAF, Immobile Branch, December 1918
4: Assistant Administrator, Grade 9, WRAF, 1918

E

1: RNAS Pilot, 1916
2: Captain Lanoe Hawker VC, 24 Squadron RFC, 1916
3: Lieutenant, RFC, trainee pilot, 1915

1

2

3

1: RAF Air Gunner, 1918
2: RAF Officer, 1918
3: Balloon Observer, Royal Artillery attached RFC, 1917

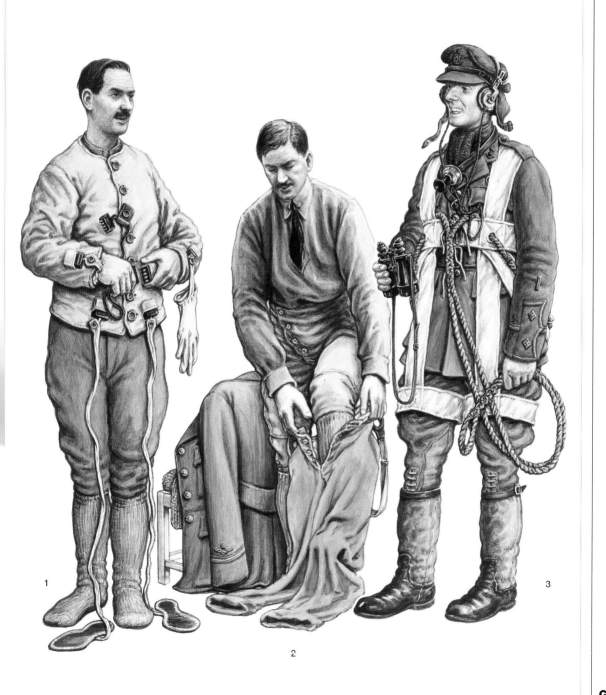

1

2

3

1: Second Lieutenant (Observer) Adrian Weller, 35 Squadron RAF, 1918
2: Sergeant Observer Reginald Murray, 202 Squadron RAF, 1918
3: RNAS/RAF Officer Pilot, 1917–18

1

2

3

Headgear

Flying helmets appeared in three forms, as caps, hoods or **protective helmets**. The French Roold helmet was accepted for issue and sealed as a pattern in May 1914 (Ptn No. 8061). It consisted of an inner skull cap surmounted by a high, domed outer hemisphere, both made of cork and gutta-percha. The space between the two was filled with special metal shavings above an inflatable rubber diaphragm. Their junction was covered by a turban of sponge rubber from which a stiff peak and a curtain covering the ears and rear of the head emerged. All outer surfaces were covered with khaki or black 'Loreid' washable fabric. The English Warren helmet (Ptn No. 8115, August 1914) used a similar double skin construction, the outer being cork and the inner thin steel plates connected to a sprung aluminium diaphragm at the apex of the dome. The two layers were separated by padding. The steel shell was held off the head by an adjustable inner leather cap. A padded brim merged into ear flaps which became a broad chin strap. The covering was brown leather-cloth. Though learners found the shock-absorbing properties of these helmets reassuring, their brims made them difficult to wear with goggles and their bulk induced drag, which made keeping a look-out a wearisome business when flying in combat. By 1915 they were used for training only, but not entirely abandoned, as a replacement pattern for both types was sealed as Helmet, Aviation (Ptn. No. 9276) in autumn 1916.

Although woollen **balaclava helmets** had been used for flying from the earliest times it seems that it was not until 1916 that a leather version was produced. The garment's face aperture was adjustable by buckled straps at the upper corners and by a cord and strap which passed round the back of the head. The type was formed as a flaired cowl extending over the wearer's shoulders and upper chest and was intended to be retained within the collar of the body garment. This mode of wear restricted the aviator's ability to turn his head somewhat, and in consequence cowls are more usually seen worn by observers, who traversed their whole body within their gun rings in order to look in the direction required. The type remained in use until the end of the war.

The most popular form was the **cap-type flying helmet** deriving from motoring caps. They were soft leather, close-fitting garments enclosing the ears, part of the cheeks and extending either to the base of the skull or further down the neck. They were lined with chamois leather, woollen or silk cloth, fur or a combination of these materials. Some had a fold-up peak, often fur covered, which could be raised or lowered as required. Ear flaps were usually provided, fitted with press-studs enabling them to be worn closed or rolled forwards; sometimes allowing the ears to protrude through the sides of the helmet. Many helmets were also made with short, vertical, stuffed cylindrical wind deflectors in front of the ear flaps. Up until 1917 some caps fastened with long lappets ending in cotton tapes, the right lappet slit horizontally for the left one to pass through, the ends then ascending through loops on the sides of the cap to tie in a bow on top of the head. The RFC sealed as patterns Caps, Fur-lined, Temporary (Ptn. No. 8150) in November 1914 and, as a replacement to 8150, Caps, Leather in May 1915 (Ptn. No. 8402), though their precise forms are uncertain. On 6 February 1917 Caps, Leather, Winter (Ptn No. 9302) and Summer (9303) were approved, having been sealed on 18 December 1916. Due to the absence of stores vocabulary numbers stamped onto garments the difference between these two patterns is uncertain. The designation according to season implies that whilst externally the same, the winter version was more fully lined with fur than the summer one. However, surviving examples of late war flying caps exhibit no significant differences; all consist of a chestnut leather outer with ear flaps and deflectors, a chamois-lined crown and a fur-lined face aperture and peak. The fastening was a simple strap and buckle under the chin. The two styles were resealed as 9407 and 9408 on 29 March, but this probably only represented a change in the sizes in which they were made. It is possible that the winter cap was not a cap-type helmet at all but was, in fact, the cowl helmet described above which provided added protection to the lower face and neck. The summer cap was certainly later renamed by the RAF as the Flying Helmet Mk. I.

Increasingly from 1915 wireless telegraphy came into use in aircraft for communicating with artillery batteries. Observers transmitted Morse code messages groundwards, but were not equipped with receivers and therefore did not require helmets carrying earphones. The introduction of air-to-air or air-to-ground wireless telephony – voice radio – led to the production of caps incorporating telephone pockets over the ears and an external extension of the chin strap which passed round the head to clamp the telephones to the ears. Alternatively, earphones were worn slotted onto elastic straps with fur chin pieces so that they could be worn with the Summer/Mk. I cap, the earphones being retained within the press-studded flaps. The earliest manual covering this equipment was

Although a posed ground shot this picture shows the terribly exposed position, both to slipstream and enemy fire, of an FE2 gunner using the rear gun mounting. The front mounting gave no more cover. No safety harness was available until very late in the war. (RAFM P4800)

Flight Sub-Lieutenant Frank Fowler in a strapped sheepskin flying coat, Chingford 1915. (RAFM Riddiford Albums)

published in October 1917. By the end of the war about 600 sets of wireless equipment had been manufactured, though telephone-equipped helmets rarely show up in photographs.

Goggles

Almost all aviators wore goggles and the aviation press strongly recommended their use. The Triplex Safety Glass Company produced several types and advertised them with testimonials as to their effectiveness. Styles with oval, round or pear-shaped windows were available, the glass being bonded to xylonite sheets which prevented its splintering in the event of a blow. Their own designs consisted of light metal frames with spring-loaded fabric sides to prevent misting up and a chenille or velvet sealing strip, the whole retained by an elastic strap. Triplex windows were also fitted into many designs of frames or masks produced by aviation kit suppliers. Numerous different designs of goggles appear in photographs and other types of window were produced including early types of celluloid plastic, like Nonflamoid made by the London Label Company, as well as very dangerous plain glass examples.

The first RFC issue goggles seem to have been made with an all rubber frame and an elastic strap. They appear frequently in the Royal Aero Club photographs of pupil pilots, particularly Other Ranks of the RFC, who would have used issue kit. By the autumn of 1915 these were relegated to use by mechanical transport drivers only. Early in 1915 a Triplex goggle mask was sealed for issue with different 'glasses', set No.1 being for pilots and No.2 for observers (Ptns Nos 8235 and 8236). These were replaced by similarly designated items in March 1916, but also by a non-tinted set of glasses. It seems likely that the patterns mentioned above were pale and dark tinted, the former available to pilots, who required less glare protection as they were looking at instruments and maps within the cockpit and benefited in many cases from the shade provided by the upper wing of their machines, and the latter for observers, who were almost constantly searching the skies for enemy aircraft. Tinting was normally yellow and the degree of density used was doubtless a matter of choice for either crew member, some not requiring any, hence the non-tinted set. In December 1916 a further mask was introduced with a protective nose piece, which indicates that the 1915 model left the nose uncovered. The 1916 Pattern was almost certainly the Triplex AB Aero Mask bought in from the trade.

This mask appears later to have been given the designation Goggle Mask Mk. I. It employed asymmetrical, pear-shaped Triplex windows in metal frames set in a fur-lined, brown leather, roughly oval mask extending about 1½ inches beyond the frames. It was retained by an adjustable elastic head band or sometimes by cotton-covered metal spring strapping. During 1918 a mask marked and described as Mk. II came into use. The designation is inexplicable because there was no difference at all between the two masks.

Oxygen equipment

The respiratory problem of breathing enough oxygen at altitude due to the decrease in atmospheric pressure was known before the First World War, but the effects of oxygen starvation were little understood. As the

operational ceilings of aircraft rose the problem was soon encountered, though solutions for small scout aircraft were beyond the technology of the day. The first RFC oxygen equipment introduced in 1917 was designed by the Siebe-Gorman Company and designated the Aero Oxygen Breathing Mask Mk. I. It was a cone of rubberised fabric, sealed with an edge of chenille and velvet, and lined in sheet rubber with an aluminium cup at its apex. The cup was fitted with louvres and an inlet tube and the mask was retained by elastic straps round the head and from the bridge of the nose over the head. Oxygen from high-pressure cylinders flowed through a regulator by narrow-bore rubber tubing. On de Havilland DH4 bombers the cylinders were carried beneath the fuselage.

Another mask, probably the one manufactured by the Dunhill flying clothing company, was issued with a radio telephony helmet. The latter, made in very dark brown leather, was fitted with lace-up telephone holders and attachment points for an oxygen mask, which was also made of leather, fur-lined and with an aluminium nose cup capable of being fitted with a microphone. This ensemble seems to be the equipment referred to in AMWO 726 of 25 July 1918 and was therefore definitely in use before the war ended. A very similar helmet, though usually fitted with a throat microphone, was used in large Handley Page V1500 machines fitted with inter-communication facilities between the crew positions. These aircraft did not become operational during the war, however.

Clothing

For most of the war the usual garment worn by aviators was a leather coat of some type. They were produced by numerous manufacturers in brown

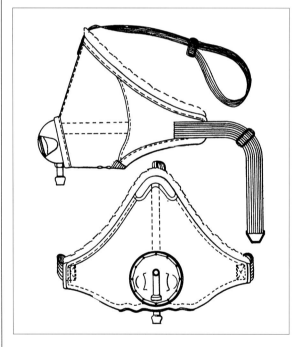

TOP **The Oxygen Breathing Mask Mk.I being adjusted on an Observer of an RFC DH4 squadron. This seems to be the only known photograph of this equipment. (IWM Neg. Q 10262)**

ABOVE **The Oxygen Breathing Mask Mk.I. Creamy-white rubber mask with aluminium nose cup, black or brown chenille and velvet sealing strip, and brown elastic straps.**

and black and with innumerable variations in length, buttoning arrangements, pockets, linings and collars. In addition it is clear that firms issued patterns so that flyers could have garments made incorporating their own modifications. Alongside leather coats, some were produced in fabric, usually closely woven proofed gabardine in shades of mid-brown. In May 1915 the RNAS introduced a 'Blue overcoat of special pattern with belt' to be worn as flying kit. It was an almost knee-length, double-breasted reefer coat with very large flap and button skirt pockets, a falling collar and shoulder straps. Officers who transferred to the RFC while in France had, per force, to wear standard greatcoats until they could re-kit themselves, and some aviators in both services wore fur coats or jackets as advertised by Spicer & Sons of Leamington Spa in *The Aeroplane* magazine.

The RFC's first official body garment, introduced in 1912, was a mid-thigh length jacket with a cross-over chest piece, two flapped pockets occupying the whole front skirt and a small, angled map pocket with flap on the chest. It fastened down the right side with visible buttons and had a stand collar fastening with two small buttons. It was lined with camel-coloured woollen fabric. An improved version with a larger, unflapped map pocket and 'grip studs' on the skirt pocket flaps was introduced in September 1913, accompanied by leather trousers with a front flap opening, buttoning to a waistband, and with buckled straps round the ankles.

These garments remained the only official body clothing until August 1916, when 'Coats, Waterproof, Pilots' were introduced. These were fabric garments, presumably of a standard raincoat-type design, lined with 'thibet' or 'slink', the very dense, curly haired/wool pelts of still-born calves/lambs respectively.

During the winter of 1916 a major development took place in flying clothing, seemingly by accident. Flight Sub-Lieutenant Sidney Cotton of 3 Wing RNAS discovered that his grease-impregnated maintenance overall was impermeable to air and gave greater protection against cold than most purpose-made flying clothing. He adapted the principle and with the assistance of J. Evans of Robinson and Cleaver Limited a design was made up consisting of an outer layer of proofed khaki twill over a rubbered muslin inter-lining and a mohair liner. The garment was a combination suit with a buttoned central fly below the waist and an externally buttoned chest flap fastening on the right. The wrists and ankles had buttoned cuffs; large open pockets were provided above each knee and it had a fur collar. Private trials proved Cotton's design and the suit became commercially available in March 1917, when it had a small, vertical flap and button left breast pocket. It was adopted by the War Office and sealed as Pattern 9686 on 10 December 1917, by which time it had probably acquired the large angled map pocket across the chest. Cotton had named the suit the Sidcot and it became the classic flying suit of the late war period; indeed, Air Ministry Order 235 of May 1918 stipulated that air crews posted abroad from training units in the UK had to be equipped with them and not leather gear.

Crew of HM Airship C4, Flt Lt Ernest Frost, Captain: Howden, early 1918. Note the different styles of goggles and the varied linings to the Sidcot suits. (RAFM DB 19)

The Sidcot was not the first overall flying suit; they had been in use since before the war, made in either leather or fabric, and they continued to be available as private purchase items throughout the period. It was, however, the most effective and remained in RAF service until 1930.

Electrically heated clothing

By 1917 the problem of cold was being addressed with the issue of electrically heated garments. Admiralty Weekly Order 2973 of August 1917 announced that 600 sets were shortly to become available to the RNAS and AdWO 4643 of December detailed their distribution to various Home and Overseas units. The RFC adopted the clothing at the same time. The RNAS set was made by the Dowsing Radiant Heat Co. Ltd and consisted of a buttoned chamois leather sleeved waistcoat providing heat to the body with cotton gloves plugging into the cuffs and retained by a buttoned tab to prevent disconnection. Foot warmth was provided by fibre inner soles glazed on their upper surface, placed within the flying boots and connected by cables and security tabs to the front hem of the waistcoat. Power to the set was provided by a windmill-driven generator attached to the aircraft structure and introduced by a four-pin terminal in the lower left front of the jacket. A switch box allowed the garments to work in combination or separately.

An almost identical set of clothing was made by The Radio Clothing Co. Ltd but in gabardine lined in fleece, and this may have been preferred by the RFC.

Electrically heated clothing was prone to malfunction due to lack of flexibility in its wiring and sometimes caused burns to its wearers due to racing of the electrical generator as the aircraft dived.

LEFT **RFC aviator in leather coat and boots and a Boddy Pattern life preserver. Note the round goggles and the lanyard, perhaps to a pistol in his left pocket. (RAFM PC 73/40/8)**

RIGHT **'McGregor blowing up Clark's Gieve waistcoat before flying to Mudros, 22 January 1918.' (RAFM PC1996/296)**

All sorts of inner garments – waistcoats, cardigans, paper clothing, chamois leather pantaloons – as well as scarves were available from commercial sources, and the RFC sealed a 'Sweater, Aviators, Temporary' in December 1914. Sweaters, Aviation continue to appear in the RAF kit lists up to 1920. Their precise form is unknown.

Gloves

The difficulties of protecting the hands from cold while allowing them the maximum sensitivity in the performance of delicate tasks posed a thorny problem and it seems to have been left very much to individuals to choose what suited them. Gauntlets with wrist straps and large cuffs were almost universal, though whether they were all leather, fur-backed, fur- or fabric-lined was left to the purchaser. Some aviators wore mittens, but they can only have been useful in training when guns and other equipment did not need to be handled. A compromise was a mitten with an independent index finger which permitted finger and thumb to work together. Another was a gauntlet glove with a supplementary fleece-lined mitten compartment for the fingers stitched across the back of the hand which could be folded back and clipped out of the way when dexterity was required. This design had been patented by a Mr. H. Urwick in 1907 (4142/1907) for general use, but was taken up by the Fownes Glove Company amongst others for aviation use. Thin inner gloves of fabric or leather were often worn so that the outer layer could be taken off when necessary. The wise airman linked his gauntlets to a long 'idiot string' threaded through the sleeves of his coat so that it was impossible to lose one when it was taken off. By 1918 gloves of silk, worsted and chamois leather are listed in kit vocabularies with different gauntlets for pilots and observers, though what the differences were is not specified.

Footwear

It seems that no special flying boots were deemed necessary in the RFC until October 1914, when a Temporary Pattern, 8137, was sealed as Boots, Knee. These were quickly replaced by an improved pattern, longer in the leg, the following month. Notes in the file indicate that these were items bought in from trade. Photographs and an example suggest that this boot had a brown, square-toed, leather foot and a suede leg with a buckled leather band at the top to close a small pleat. The whole was lined in white sheepskin. This type of boot turns up so frequently in photographs worn by air crew of all ranks that it is most likely to be an issue garment.

Also in November 1914 'Overshoes, Gaitered' received Pattern No. 8147 and they continue to appear throughout the war in kit lists. It seems likely that these were black waterproof fabric boots, loose all down the leg to permit the passage of a shoed foot and fastening round the ankle and in-step with a panel and three straps. The sole and foot part was formed as a rubber galosh and the shaped top was bound in leather.

Despite these issue items many aviators seem to have flown in ordinary marching boots or field boots, but increased altitude and cold eventually became a significant problem. Practical experience again came to the rescue when Major Lanoe Hawker VC, DSO, designed a thigh-length sheepskin boot with leather foot and had it made up by Harrods Ltd. Tried out in service conditions by 24 Squadron, the

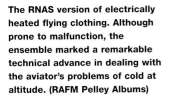

The RNAS version of electrically heated flying clothing. Although prone to malfunction, the ensemble marked a remarkable technical advance in dealing with the aviator's problems of cold at altitude. (RAFM Pelley Albums)

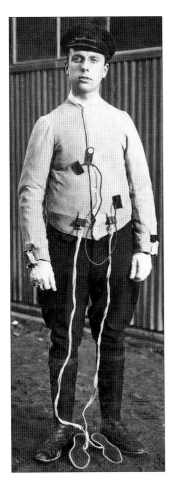

Sergeant Frederick Cecil Crespin, Observer/Gunner of one of 217 Squadron's DH4 bombers, 1918. He wears the Sidcot suit with Perrin/Auliff life preserver, the summer pattern helmet and Goggles Mk. I. (RAFM PC1998/74/1)

Charfor, as Harrods called it, quickly became known as the 'fug boot'. It had buckled leather retaining straps at the ankle and below the knee and an adjustable suspension strap at the top intended to engage with a button at waist level. The type was sealed as Boots, Thigh in December 1916 and it seems that the leather foot was reduced to a toe cap and a heel piece. Surviving examples have thick red rubber soles. Other commercially supplied copies were without leather additions at all and some versions seem to have had a rubber galosh foot. A knee-length version was officially supplied, probably for wear inside combination suits, though some examples of these were certainly thigh boots cut down.

As with all flying kit, footwear was available commercially, though much was worn inside other garments and is therefore invisible in photographs. Very few outfitters' advertisements illustrate footwear.

SAFETY EQUIPMENT

Life preservers

Experiments with hydro-aeroplanes – float planes – in pre-war days had proved that flying over and landing on water was possible, potentially advantageous and dangerous; fragile airframes and temperamental engines ensured that aviators often ended up in the water. The problem first presented itself to the RFC in its initial passage to France in August 1914, and it was a continuing problem thereafter due to the regular requirement to send replacement machines to the British Expeditionary Force. The pioneers of these ferrying flights put their faith in tyre inner tubes to keep them afloat, but somewhat more sophisticated life preservers had been available since at least 1910. The RNAS was, naturally, more familiar with the hazard. Both forces addressed the problem with different equipment, all of it drawn from commercial suppliers.

One device was invented by George Mallory Boddy of Boddy Life Saving Appliances (1914) Limited (UK Patent 11,337/1914). It consisted of three linked pads of kapok 'buoyant vegetable wool', a medium-sized one across the shoulders, a large one on the chest and a small one at waist level, retained in position by tapes from the lower rear corners passing under the arms and tying between the two front panels. It was designed to keep the wearer afloat and face upwards with the head well out of the water. A second version, Patent 5197/1915, divided the front two panels vertically so that the device fitted better round the body; the lower panel was also fastened round the waist with a tape. This design was known as the Boddy No.5 jacket and was sealed as a Pattern for the RFC (No. 8652) in February 1916, though it had been in use long before that. Its issue was restricted to air crew below 5 feet 9 inches in height.

Mr. Boddy had also invented a jacket as early as August 1912 which achieved the same distribution of kapok flotation cells within a fairly normal-looking belted, sleeved jacket fastening from hem to throat with seven large buttons. It featured two flap and button breast pockets. Kapok pads or quilting had the added advantage of providing some thermal insulation to the wearer and some buffering effect in the event of a crash.

Mr. H. H. Read of Falmouth manufactured a belted Norfolk jacket in blue twill or khaki made from a buoyant fabric patented in the United States (US Patent 895,480, August 1908) by Niels Mathias Mathesen, a

Dane. The fabric consisted of cotton wool held between an outer fabric and a lining, the cotton wool having been 'saturated throughout... with a vapour impregnated with an oily substance'. Anyone wearing clothing made from this fabric would be 'buoyant for an ordinarily sufficient length of time to float... until he is rescued', though the fabric was admitted not to be permanently water-repelling. The single-breasted, tunic-length jacket had internal leather flaps fastening with clips across the chest and double lined sleeves with storm cuffs. In the extraordinarily solitary circumstances likely to be encountered by downed airmen it was probably of questionable efficacy. It was sealed for the RFC as Pattern No. 8653 in February 1916 and was to be issued to men of 5 feet 9 inches and over in height.

Messieurs Gieve, Matthews & Seagrove Limited patented a conventional waistcoat in November 1914 (22,267/1914) which incorporated a rubber bladder held discretely within a tube of fabric around the wearer's lower chest. When buttoned up and orally inflated by a valved tube concealed in the left breast pocket the effect was like a child's bathing ring. A glass flask for spirits was supplied with the garment, which was made up in khaki twill or dark blue serge. The device would keep a body afloat, but not necessarily with the face out of the water. A development of this jacket dispensed with the ring and provided linked inflatable bladders conforming in shape to the front halves of the garment.

The most sophisticated and convenient 'life jacket' of the period was the 'Perrin Arm Brace' first mentioned in *The Aeroplane* on 28 August 1913. Designed by Paul Perrin, a Frenchman, the agency for the device in the UK was in the hands of a Mr. Mark Auliff. The design was patented in France by Patent number 406,020 of July 1909 and improvements were covered in Patent number 411,874 of January 1910. By the time it was adopted by the RNAS these original designs had undergone refinements, probably at the hands of Mr. Auliff.

As worn by the RNAS the life preserver consisted of a rectangular rubberised-fabric bladder linked in front by two triangular D rings and snap hooks and supported over the shoulders by adjustable braces. In the lower left side a housing was formed to accommodate a compressed liquid-gas cylinder which inflated the bladder when operated by a lever. Photographs indicate that an oral inflation valve was provided on the upper right corner. In its deflated condition the dull yellow-orange bladder hung slackly round the body just below the armpits; in its inflated state, it formed a ring round the upper torso with forward extensions designed to ensure the wearer floated face upwards. Stores vocabularies compiled in or after 1918 mention both Perrin and Auliff life preservers as if they were two similar though different equipments. It seems likely, however, that manufacturers' labels or custom and practice lead to the adoption of both names to describe identical items.

Flight Lieutenant (Observer) Eric Bourne Coulter Betts, 2 Naval Squadron/202 Squadron RAF, beside his DH4 at Dunkirk, 1918. He wears a private purchase flying suit, short sheepskin boots and the Perrin/Auliff life belt. (RAFM Box 125)

RAF vocabularies also include a Leavy life saving device about which nothing is known and, of course, other life preservers were available for private purchase including examples from the General Aeronautical Company. As the Read, Gieve and the Boddy jackets, but not the Boddy No.5 device, were usually worn under flying kit there is almost no photographic evidence of their use.

PARACHUTES AND HARNESSES

Leonardo da Vinci is credited with designing the first parachute in the early 16th century, and during the 19th century demonstration descents were made from balloons using canopies which were usually deployed on frames before the drop was made. During the First World War the crews of aeroplanes were not provided with these devices, partly because of the disadvantage of carrying the extra weight and partly because the authorities seem not to have trusted the occupants only to use them in dire emergencies. This distrust was not extended to kite balloon observers, who were sitting targets once machine-gun armed aeroplanes started using incendiary ammunition. The RNAS also authorised the carriage of one parachute per man in airships by AdWO 2552 of July 1917.

At this period no convenient packaging had been devised which allowed a man to carry his canopy with him, nor was there any sure means of deploying the canopy satisfactorily once the equipment was separated from its aerial anchorage point. Both common parachute types – the Spencer and the Calthrop/Guardian Angel – held the canopy separately attached to the balloon or airship structure, and relied upon the weight of the man to drag the canopy out of its container. The technicalities of guaranteeing a successful deployment are outside the scope of this book, but suffice it to say that the Spencer used a pack in the form of a truncated cone 27 inches long, with its 15-inch diameter 'mouth' at the lower end; the Guardian Angel used a slightly convex cylindrical pack 24 inches in diameter by 7 inches thick. Usually a single rope line attached the crewman to the canopy line by means of a snap hook, a shackle or a knot. An elastic shock-absorbing cord was normally incorporated in the canopy line.

Harnesses seem to have been extremely crude and, though obviously strong enough for their purpose, took little account of the ergonomic distribution of the loads on the wearer's body at the moment of deceleration when the canopy deployed fully. The most primitive was made solely from rope spliced together in various loops

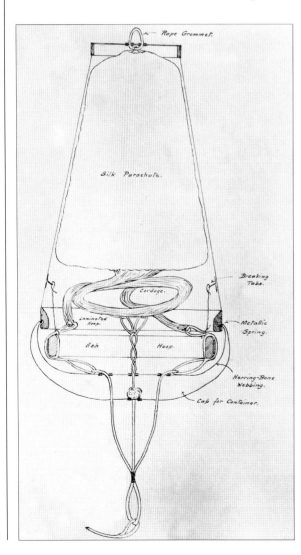

The Spencer parachute packed in its valise. The connection line to the wearer's harness depended from a wooden hoop to which the canopy shrouds were also connected. The mouth of the valise was formed by a plywood ring against which the lower, outer cover of the pack was clamped by a metallic spring. Canopy deployment was achieved by the in-rush of air as the canopy was dragged out of the container. (RAFM Pelley Albums)

so as to provide a figure-of-eight harness around the arms and across the chest and shoulders with another similar arrangement linked to it around the upper legs. The suspension line emerged from the chest so that when descending the wearer held onto it to keep himself in a sitting position. Most other harnesses seem to have been made from very wide white cotton webbing with rope acting as the main load bearing element, either sewn directly to it or retained within narrow webbing sewn to the broader strips to form sleeves. The suspension point of these types was either on the chest or between the shoulders. By 1918 slightly more sophis-

One of the more sophisticated designs of parachute harness, permitting easy adjustment of the strap lengths to ensure a comfortable fit. The suspension point from between the shoulders permits no chance of control during the descent, however. (RAFM P015842 & 3)

ticated harnesses with adjustment buckles and chest-mounted release bosses were undergoing trials.

As most kite balloon observers wore long leather flying coats they were obliged to wear their harnesses inside them. Some airship officers provided themselves with combination flying suits and could therefore wear theirs over their outer clothing. In fact the generally low altitudes at which airships operated, and the instinct to stay with the ship no matter what happened, mean that it is extremely rare to see photographs of RNAS airship personnel wearing harnesses. Despite this the RNAS seems to have conducted more experiments with parachutes than the RFC.

BIBLIOGRAPHY

Air Force Memorandum No. 2, Dress Regulations for the Royal Air Force
Air Ministry Weekly and Monthly Orders, 1918 & 1919
Field Service Publication No. 7, Provisional Instructions regarding Non-Technical Supplies and Services
Field Service Publication No. 14, Constitution and Regulations of the WRAF
Field Service Publication No. 18, Voluntary Transfer of ... WRNS, WAAC and Women's Legion Motor Drivers to the WRAF
Field Service Publication No. 32, Uniform for the WRAF
Admiralty Air Dept Publication No. 27, Electrically Heated Clothing ...
Air Publication 64, ... Intercommunication Telephones on Handley Page Machines...
Air Publication 109, Telephone, Wireless, Aircraft, Mk.II

THE PLATES

A1: Lieutenant, RAF, spring 1918

Based on a photograph of Lieutenant Geoffrey Barfoot-Saunt, this figure wears the khaki officer's uniform of 1918 with a woollen cardigan beneath. Rank bars appear on the cap band, and his belt has a single-prong buckle with retaining loop often seen on early uniforms. A gold wound stripe is worn. Barfoot-Saunt served as an Engineering Branch Staff Officer and continued to wear the old RFC Staff Officer's armband Pattern 1915.

A2: Captain, RAF, Medical Officer, winter 1918-1919

Cuff eagles and cap band rank bars had been abolished on blue kit by the time it was permitted as Service Dress day wear. Medical Officers were distinguished by a maroon cap band and the large Crux Anasata collar badges from October 1918. This figure wears War Service chevrons indicating service from 1914 onwards.

A3: Second Lieutenant, RAF, spring 1918

Difficulties in procuring the new RAF uniform and the need for economy resulted in some adapted dress being acceptable for a short period. This Officer commissioned in January has acquired one of the RAF 'war economy' cap badges for his RFC SD cap; he has removed the pips from his jacket shoulder straps and added eagle and crown badges to his cuffs. He has not been able to change the badges on his waterproof coat, but has acquired a black tie.

Otherwise he wears exactly what he expected to wear when he joined the RFC in 1917.

B1: Air Mechanic 1st Class, Wireless Mechanic, late spring 1918

This AM1 is wearing the Pattern 1918 Version 1 airmen's jacket announced in Air Force Memorandum No. 2. Although the buttons and buckle are described as being of bronze, photographs and an example clearly indicate that they were of gilding metal. The pattern in the RAF Museum collection has no buttons on the lower pocket flaps, but issued jackets certainly had them. The jacket is rarely seen in photographs and does not seem to have been widely issued. The lower pockets and buckle must have made it relatively expensive to manufacture. Only Air Mechanics 1st Class wore their trade badges below their rank badges.

B2: Corporal, RAF Police, 1919

The Jacket, Pattern 1918, Version 2 with leather buttons and buttoned belt was much more widely issued than the first version and remained in use as working dress until about 1923. The inset skirt pockets required no buttons on the flaps. This figure wears the gilding metal cap badge of May 1919 and the arm band of the RAF Police Department introduced in September 1918, plus a whistle on a chain.

B3: Bandsman, 1918

Few RAF personnel were issued with the pale blue uniform, but No.1 RAF Band certainly had it by July 1918. The early-style shoulder eagles have a much more elegant curve

LEFT **Officers and men of 141 Squadron, Ireland, 1918. Whilst both Warrant Officers wear eagle rank insignia on the arm they wear different cap badges, though both have the second version of the WOI's jacket. The Airmen wear both versions of the 1918 Pattern jacket with buckled and buttoned belts. The figure at middle row far left appears to have a small metal eagle on his cap badge. All clothing is khaki. (RAFM PC71/19/36/4)**

OPPOSITE **Officers' Mess at Imbros, Eastern Mediterranean, 1918. RAF and RNAS Khaki and KD clothing is worn. A Civil Branch officer in whites is also shown. Note the RAF lace on the cuffs, the bronze pips on the shoulder straps, the mixture of cap badges and the continued use of Sam Brownes. (RAFM Photo Box 41)**

to their wings than later examples and the impressive lyre badge seems to have been completely unofficial.

C1: Warrant Officer Class I/Sergeant Major, summer 1918

WOIs wore a uniform very similar to that of the officers with the same jacket, cap and badge. Their rank was very discreetly shown on the upper arm. On the few occasions when pistol equipment was required they continued to wear the Sam Browne as they had in the RFC, though they had no shoulder straps to retain the brace.

C2: Warrant Officer Class II; Russian Intervention campaign, winter 1918-19

Seen immediately after leaving a medal presentation parade at which he has received the Cross of St. George 4th Class, this WOII wears the standard Other Ranks' RAF greatcoat, with headgear provided by our White Russian allies to which he has added a gold embroidered badge. On less formal occasions photographs show felt or fur snow boots being worn.

C3: Sergeant, Physical Training Instructor, autumn 1918

This NCO shows the transitional clothing many airmen found themselves wearing in place of strictly RAF uniform. His Army General Service Pattern jacket has not been converted at all, but he has managed to acquire the unofficial shoulder titles modelled on the old RFC ones. His trade is acknowledged by the new PTI's badge of crossed sabres overlaid with an eagle and surmounted by a crown. He wears a yellow embroidered cap badge which was introduced because of the shortage of gold embroidery wire.

D1: Lieutenant, RAF, formerly RNAS; Mediterranean, summer 1918

Difficulties of supply have obliged this officer to continue to wear his RNAS cap in its KD cover and with its original badge. The confusion caused by the lack of instructions on tropical dress have led to an attempt to convert his RNAS KD jacket by the removal of the shoulder straps and original cuff rank lace and their replacement with RAF lace and eagles. As the Sam Browne is no longer to be worn a belt remains a problem, but he has managed to get the RAF pilot's badge.

D2: Flight Sergeant, Egypt, 1918

Photographs indicate that Khaki Drill Field Service caps were produced for the RFC in the Middle East. This figure continues to wear his RFC badge as no suitable alternative for this headgear was available to the RAF. His rank badge has been made up using Warrant Officer II large crowns and RAF brass shoulder titles have been commissioned from the local bazaar. He is in the process of lowering and binding in the legs of his shorts as the evening mosquito hazard comes on. He continues to wear the Army four-pocket KD tunic, though the RAF Jacket Pattern 1918 Version 2 as shown in Figure B2 was also produced in KD and gradually came into use.

D3: Captain, RAF, formerly RFC; Egypt/Palestine, 1918

This officer has removed the metal rank pips from his shoulder straps and replaced them with RAF khaki and pale blue lace. He has also removed his RFC collar badges and adopted a black tie. Apart from those minor changes, and having been awarded the Distinguished Flying Cross, he wears exactly the same kit as before 1 April 1918.

E1: Chief Section Leader, WRAF, Motor Transport, winter 1918

Wearing the single-breasted jacket in pale blue with the elaborate badge of her rank, this NCO has also been issued with the Cap, Motor Transport Drivers. She wears long laced boots, privately purchased scarf and ocelot fur gauntlets, and holds a pair of 'Goggles, Mechanical Transport Drivers' which were the first issue pattern of RFC rubber flying goggles relegated to MT use.

E2: Sister, RAF Nursing Service, outdoor uniform, October 1918

The outdoor uniform consisted of the uniform dress with the

Norfolk jacket worn over it. In the absence of photographic evidence collar badges are shown in the conventional position and the hat badge is mounted on the hat band, whose bow is invisible at the side of the hat. The RAFNS appears to have worn white gloves.

E3: Sub-Leader, WRAF, Immobile Branch, December 1918

It seems to have been a matter of personal preference as to which of the two jacket styles Members wore. The flap-over type was reminiscent of the RFC jacket of 1912; its belt fastened in line with the opening. The array of badges worn by this member of the Immobile Branch was only possible between December 1918 and February 1919 when, according to regulations, the WRAF shoulder title was suppressed.

E4: Assistant Administrator, Grade 9, WRAF, 1918

WRAF officers were recruited directly or transferred into the service from the WAAC or the WRNS. Their rank insignia were distinctly different from those of their male colleagues until December 1918, when the buttons indicating rank were abolished and gilt crowned eagles were substituted. The change had been anticipated in the 'Constitution and Regulations of the WRAF' published in November.

F1: RNAS Pilot, 1916

Many RNAS officers opted for black flying coats instead of brown, and they were often cut double-breasted like their uniforms rather than being in the flap-over style favoured by the RFC. The other elements are all typically private purchase

styles. Uniform field boots and breeches complete the flying outfit. The RNAS does not seem to have developed a range of official issue clothing for its airmen, perhaps because relatively few of them were Ratings needing issued kit.

F2: Captain Lanoe Hawker VC, 24 Squadron, 1916

Hawker wears a private purchase fur coat over the leather trousers with ankle straps from the 1913 two-piece flying suit – see F3 for the jacket. His boots are the official issue Boots, Knee, Temporary of 1914 with leather foot and suede leg – see G3. Hawker seems to have worn a very baggy balaclava helmet over his leather helmet, but for clarity's sake this is deleted. He certainly wore the official issue red rubber goggles of 1914.

F3: Lieutenant, RFC, trainee pilot, 1915

Based on a photograph of Lieutenant Wyndham Levy Grech, this figure shows the 1913 Pattern short RFC flying jacket, a private purchase helmet and a pair of Featherweight Triplex goggles. This officer wears what are believed to be 'Overshoes, Gaitered' introduced in 1914 and which continued to appear in kit lists until the end of the war. Little photographic evidence of them is available, but some variants appear to fasten with metal clasps instead of buckles.

G1: RAF Air Gunner, 1918

Both the RFC and the RNAS introduced electrically heated clothing in late 1917, though it seems to have been restricted to multi-seat aircraft.

G2: RAF Officer, 1918

Numerous items of theoretically useful flying clothing were available for private purchase. Chamois leather pantaloons gave extra protection to the legs, but could only be worn inside trousers, not breeches, because of the restriction at the knee. Woollen underwear provided the foundation layer and a sweater or cardigan an intermediate layer between shirt and jacket. The normal uniform garments had to be worn under flying kit to assure the wearer of the protection of the Geneva Convention in the event of capture.

G3: Balloon Observer, Royal Artillery attached RFC, 1917

Shown without his leather flying coat, this 'balloonatic' wears Service Dress with a parachute harness in broad cotton webbing. His 'Gor' Blimey' cap provides better eye shading than a flying helmet and adequate warmth. To communicate with the ground he wears earphones and has a microphone suspended round his neck. His flying boots are the Boots, Knee, Temporary of 1914.

H1: Second Lieutenant (Observer) Adrian Weller, 35 Squadron RAF, 1918

Universal from 1915 to at least spring 1918, the long leather flying coat came with many minor variations. Weller wears a private purchase helmet which fastens with press studs across the chin, and the Mk.I Goggle Mask. He has attached his map board and another item to strings not only to prevent their being blown away but to stop them falling into the bottom of his Armstrong Whitworth FK8 aircraft and jamming the control cables.

Flight Sub-Lieutenant Marmaduke Marsden wearing a double-breasted, short black leather flying coat with RNAS gilt buttons, fur collar and, most unusually, shoulder straps with gold rank lace and eagle. (RAFM Manton Album)

LEFT **Flight Sub-Lieutenant Warner Peberdy and Flt Lt Hugh Aird of F Squadron RNAS, Mudros, 1916. Aird wears a fur coat over leather trousers while Peberdy sports a private purchase flying suit. Both wear Perrin/Auliff type life belts. (RAFM B357)**

H2: Sergeant Observer Reginald Murray, 202 Squadron RAF, 1918

Murray wears the classic Sidcot suit/'fug boot' combination of the late war period. His gauntlets incorporate the supplementary mitten compartment to keep the fingers warm.

H3: RNAS/RAF Officer Pilot, 1917–18

This officer wears a private purchase Burberry flying suit buttoning on the left and with a tail of fabric emerging from the centre of the chest flap which encircles the neck to keep the fur collar up. He wears a helmet (RAFM 80/U/910) which sports a black cat lucky charm; several helmets in the RAF Museum collection have such personal decorations. The Perrin/Auliff life belt could be worn with the inflation cylinder on either the left or the right as the wearer found most convenient. Fur gauntlets and knee-length boots complete the outfit.

INDEX

COMPANION SERIES FROM OSPREY

CAMPAIGN
Concise, authoritative accounts of history's decisive military encounters. Each 96-page book contains over 90 illustrations including maps, orders of battle, colour plates, and three-dimensional battle maps.

WARRIOR
Definitive analysis of the appearance, weapons, equipment, tactics, character and conditions of service of the individual fighting man throughout history. Each 64-page book includes full-colour uniform studies in close detail, and sectional artwork of the soldier's equipment.

NEW VANGUARD
Comprehensive histories of the design, development and operational use of the world's armoured vehicles and artillery. Each 48-page book contains eight pages of full-colour artwork including a detailed cutaway.

ORDER OF BATTLE
The most detailed information ever published on the units which fought history's great battles. Each 96-page book contains comprehensive organisation diagrams supported by ultra-detailed colour maps. Each title also includes a large fold-out base map.

ELITE
Detailed information on the organisation, appearance and fighting record of the world's most famous military bodies. This series of 64-page books, each containing some 50 photographs and diagrams and eight full-colour plates, will broaden in scope to cover personalities, significant military techniques, and other aspects of the history of warfare which demand a comprehensive illustrated treatment.

AIRCRAFT OF THE ACES
Focuses exclusively on the elite pilots of major air campaigns, and includes unique interviews with surviving aces sourced specifically for each volume. Each 96-page volume contains up to 40 specially commissioned artworks, unit listings, new scale plans and the best archival photography available.

COMBAT AIRCRAFT
Technical information from the world's leading aviation writers on the century's most significant military aircraft. Each 96-page volume contains up to 40 specially commissioned artworks, unit listings, new scale plans and the best archival photography available.